The Buildings of Ludlow

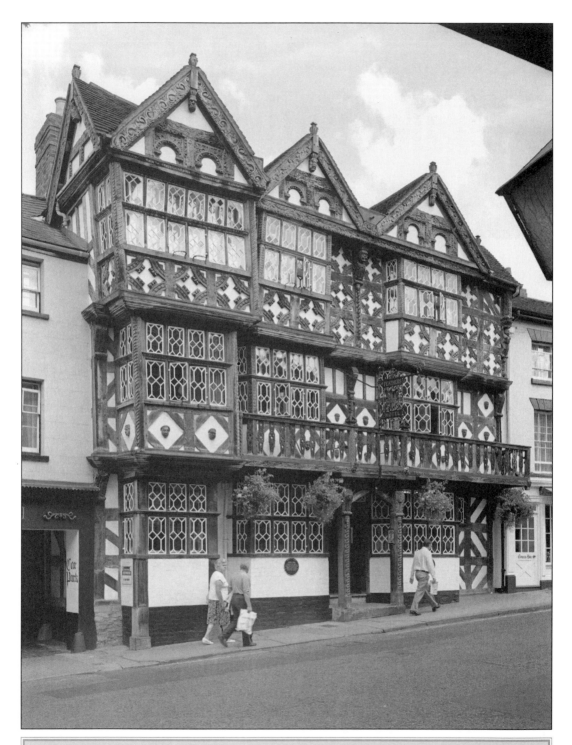

1 The spectacular Feathers Hotel, in the Bull Ring, must be one of the most famous, and most photographed, timber-framed buildings in the world. The richly carved Jacobean façade probably dates to a radical rebuilding of 1619, but the balcony is a nineteenth-century addition. In about 1670 it became an inn, and more recently has become a top-class hotel of international standing.

The Buildings of Ludlow

RICHARD K. MORRISS

With photographs by Ken Hoverd

ALAN SUTTON

First published in the United Kingdom in 1993 by
Alan Sutton Publishing Limited
Phoenix Mill · Far Thrupp · Stroud · Gloucestershire

First published in the United States of America in 1993 by
Alan Sutton Publishing Inc. · 83 Washington Street · Dover
NH 03820

British Library Cataloguing in Publication Data

Morriss, Richard K.
 Buildings of Ludlow
 I. Title
 720.94245

 ISBN 0–7509–0254–X

Library of Congress Cataloging in Publication Data applied for

*Cover illustrations: front: detail of the Feathers Hotel; inset:
William Baker's Butter Cross. Back: Ludlow Castle.*

Typeset in 11/14 Times.
Typesetting and origination by
Alan Sutton Publishing Limited.
Printed in Great Britain by
The Bath Press, Bath, Avon.

Contents

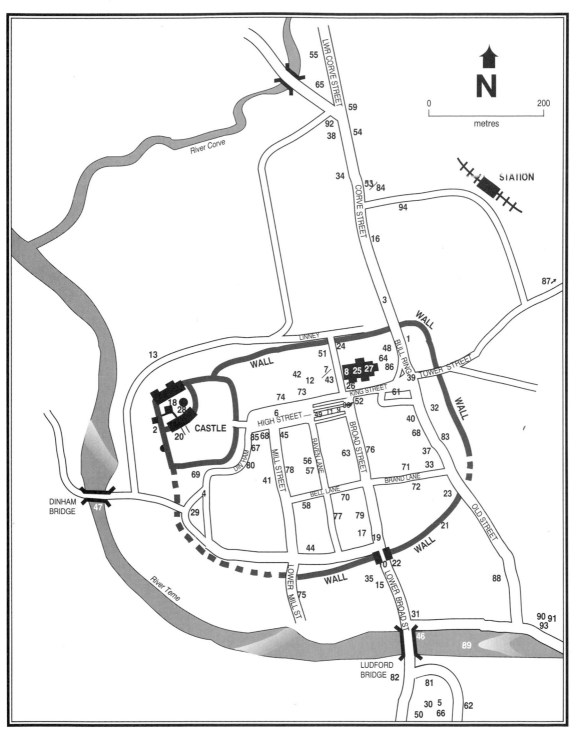

(Numbers relate to caption numbers in text)

Introduction

Our next expedition was to Ludlow, a place of fame and antiquity . . . wall'd quite round and pretty strong . . . upon a hill top . . . on which, precipitous to the north and west, stands the castle. On the south side runs the Teme, fetter'd with numerous dams across, in nature of cataracts, by which means abundance of mills are turn'd. The superfluous water pours over 'em cascade like, with a mighty noise.

(William Stukeley, 1724)

Ludlow is seen as the textbook example of a planted medieval town, laid out alongside its Norman castle. Virtually nothing is known of the earlier history of the site, for although *Lvdeford*, on the south bank of the Teme, is mentioned in the Domesday Book of 1086, Ludlow itself is not. Until recently, the river marked the boundary between the counties of Shropshire and Herefordshire, and Ludford was only incorporated fully into Shropshire in 1901.

The site of Ludlow was in a detached part of the important Saxon manor of Stanton. A few miles to the north is the Saxon church of Stanton Lacy, well worth a visit in its own right. The 'Lacy' added to that village's name belonged to the de Lacy family, friends of the Conqueror. After a Saxon uprising against the Normans in Shropshire was ruthlessly suppressed, Stanton was given to Walter de Lacy and he began building a castle on the best defensive site in his new manor – the top of cliffs overlooking the Teme at Ludlow. This was clearly seen as an important strategic base for the pacification of the turbulent borderland and was one of only a handful of Norman castles build in stone from the start. The work would have been carried on by Walter's son, Roger, after 1085 but he became involved in a rebellion against William II and was banished in 1094.

The de Lacys established a small settlement to the south of the castle, an area now called Dinham. The original castle gateway faced south, towards Dinham, and the street pattern of this area does not tie in with the slightly later planned town to the east. Dinham also had its own chapel, which may have been the original parish church. The *Fitzwarine Romance*, written in the early fourteenth century, is part-fact and part-fiction but does state that the town of Ludlow was called *Dynan* in the twelfth century.

The first mention of *Lodelowe* occurs in 1138, when it was caught up in the civil war between Stephen and Matilda and the castle was held by Joce de Dinan. In the following year the castle was besieged by Stephen in person, who is said to have rescued the young Prince Henry of Scotland from a grappling iron. It is unclear whether or not the new town had been laid out by this date, but it had probably been started by the middle of the twelfth century – by which time the de Lacys had regained control.

New towns like Ludlow were designed to serve the castle, providing, for example, a convenient source of food and manpower. More importantly, they brought all the marketing of local farm produce under the direct control of the local magnate, providing income through rents and market tolls. There were many such plantations in England, particularly up and down the mid-Wales border, but few have survived as urban settlements. Failed towns nearby include Caus, Ruyton-of-the-Eleven-Towns, Clun, and Richard's Castle.

Ludlow had a very simple, and rigid, grid pattern. Just to the north the Teme is joined by the Corve and the town occupies the ridge of high ground between the two. A wide High Street was laid out to the east of the castle on the crest of the ridge. From here, three main streets – Mill Street, Broad Street and Old Street – ran down the gentler southern slope towards the Teme. Running at right angles from them were narrow burgage plots backing on to service alleys parallel to the main streets. Halfway down the slope a cross lane running parallel to the High Street linked all three main streets. The line of Old Street continued northwards over the ridge, through the Bull Ring at the end of the High Street, and down the slope towards the Corve by Corve Street. Recent research has shown that this apparently simple pattern was not all laid out at the same time and may have taken well over a century to complete.

The wide High Street was the site of the market, but gradually the temporary tables and stalls became more and more permanent and part of the area became colonized by rows of buildings – a process known as 'market infilling'. This resulted in the very narrow streets at the east end of the former High Street – now known as Market Street, Harp Lane, High Street and Church Street – contrasting with the wider area at the west end, Castle Square. Ludlow clearly prospered as a market town but it also benefited from the Welsh wool trade. Several important wool merchants are known to have been connected with the town, the greatest of these being Lawrence of Ludlow. He was one of the wealthiest commoners in late thirteenth-century England, and built Stokesay Castle near Craven Arms. As well as trading in wool, the town also had its own woollen industry. The River Teme provided the water power, harnessed by weirs, to turn the

2 A brooding castle under a brooding sky. The cliffs overhanging the Teme were the best defensive site in the de Lacy lands, and the obvious place to build their stronghold. The view from the south has changed since the castle ceased to be defensive. Before then the land would have been kept clear of trees to avoid the risk of surprise attacks.

2 Published in 1851, this Victorian engraving of the castle shows the Great Hall range and the Norman chapel of the Inner Bailey.

waterwheels of the fulling mills that processed the raw woollen cloth. By the end of the thirteenth century the population was probably around 1,500, quite sizeable for medieval England. It was also considered important enough to be protected by town walls, parts of which survive more or less intact.

The de Lacys held Ludlow until the mid-thirteenth century when it passed, by marriage, to the de Geneville and Verdun families and then, at the start of the fourteenth century, to the infamous Roger de Mortimer. This powerful and ambitious Marcher Lord was exiled in 1323 but returned a few years later as the lover of Edward II's queen, Isabella. He made himself Earl of March, and effectively took over the kingdom. It was probably on his orders that the king was murdered at Berkeley Castle, but he was toppled in turn by the young Edward III and executed in 1330. Surprisingly, the new king forgave de Mortimer's descendants and one of his granddaughters, Phillipa, married Roger's great-grandson, Edmund, 3rd Earl of March. This alliance later led to the Wars of the Roses. The 5th Earl was lucky to escape with his head when he plotted against Henry V in 1415, claiming to be the true heir to the throne. His nephew Richard became the 6th Earl in 1425 and was also the Duke of

3 The sweeping slope of Corve Street, looking northwards, indicates just how wide the main medieval streets of the new town were. The line of Corve Street, and Old Street to the south, is considered to reflect part of an ancient trading route along the Welsh border.

York. He too claimed the throne, then held by the Lancastrian, Henry VI, and war broke out between the two factions.

Ludlow was obviously a Yorkist stronghold and was attacked by a Lancastrian army led by Henry himself in October 1459. The defending forces were weakened by the defection overnight of their best troops and gave up quickly at the Battle of Ludford. The Duke of York and his son managed to escape but both town and castle were taken and ransacked. One chronicler bemoaned the 'mysrewle of the kyngys galents . . . [for] . . . whenn they hadded dronkyn i-nowe of wyne that was in tavernys and in other placys, they full ungoodely smote owte the heddys of the pypys and hoggys hedys of wyne, that men wente wetschode in wyne, and thenn they robbed the towne, and bare a-waye bed-dynge, clothe, and other stuffe, and defoulyd many wymmen . . .'. The Lancastrian success was short-lived. Although Richard was killed at the Battle of Wakefield, his son Edward won a decisive victory in 1461 at Mortimer's Cross, near Ludlow, and went on to become Edward IV. Ludlow thus became a royal possession and was rewarded for its 'laudable and gratuitous services' to the Yorkist cause when Edward transferred his manorial rights to the 'bailiffs, burgesses and commonality' of the town, and gave it a new borough charter.

Ludlow had probably suffered some decline in the late four-teenth century because of the devastating effects of the Black Death and the decline of the raw wool trade, but by the mid-fifteenth century it was again prosperous. As well as enjoying royal patronage, Ludlow had also developed another branch of the woollen industry, weaving cloth. The town's medieval wealth is reflected in its magnificent parish church, St Laurence's, rebuilt between the 1430s and 1460s and as grand as any of the famous 'wool' churches of East Anglia. Much of the expense of the church was borne by the Palmers' Gild, a quasi-religious organization founded in the mid-thirteenth century and claiming connection with the crusaders. In many ways the Gild was a medieval self-help group. It invested heavily in property and used the profits to help its less fortunate members and the town in general, providing, for example, financial assistance, chaplains in the church, almshouses, and the first school.

Edward IV sent his two young sons, Edward and Richard, to live at the castle. With them went a group of courtiers and gentlemen,

4 A quiet corner in Dinham. This part of the town may well pre-date the rest of the town, though its origins are not very clear. It has certainly kept its individuality over the centuries.

a loosely knit council that would develop as the Council of the Welsh Marches. After the king died in 1483 the young Edward V began the long journey to London – where both he and his brother were murdered in the Tower and their uncle, Richard III, became king. Richard, the last of the Yorkist kings, was in turn defeated by Henry Tudor at Bosworth two years later, but Ludlow's royal links continued. In 1493 Henry VII's popular eldest son, Prince Arthur, was sent to Ludlow and in 1501 he brought his young bride, Catherine of Aragon, back to the castle. Sadly, the young prince died within a few months of his marriage; his heart was buried in St Laurence's. Catherine later married Arthur's brother, the new heir, who became Henry VIII in 1509. Arthur's premature death in Ludlow completely altered the course of British history. The last royal to live in the castle was Henry and Catherine's notorious daughter, 'Bloody' Mary, who spent several winters there as a young girl.

5 Ludford, south of the Teme, is older than its larger neighbour and appears in the Domesday Book. This Saxon settlement was mainly in Herefordshire until the start of the twentieth century. St Giles's Hospital (actually almshouses) lies to the east of the church of that name, while the tower of St Laurence's dominates the skyline.

Locally, the influence of the Council of the Welsh Marches was minimal until 1534 when Bishop Rowland Lee became President. He transformed it into a power base for the Crown in the borders, and Ludlow effectively became the administrative and legislative centre for most of Wales and the English border counties. Lee boasted that 'all the theves in Wales quake for feare'. The work of the Council attracted judges, lawyers, clerks, litigants and other officials to the town – as well as hangers-on. The castle itself, unlike so many others in the country, remained in use and new buildings were added to it. Many buildings still standing in the town have connections with the Council and other late sixteenth-century, timber-framed houses reflect the prosperity of the period, a time when the population probably reached 3,000. Just as the Council became important, the influence of the Palmers' Gild stopped;

as a quasi-religious organization it was a late casualty of the Dissolution, its assets and responsibilities being transferred to the borough in 1551.

From a peak at the start of the 1580s, the town's woollen industry began an accelerating decline that continued through the seventeenth century. The Council was an important factor in maintaining Ludlow's economy, but even so the population fell gradually until the Civil War. The Council was closed, despite a plea from the townspeople to the king that 'the greatest part of the Inhabitants will short time grow so poore, that they will not be able to provide maintenance for their families'.

Shropshire was mainly a Royalist county and Ludlow was held for the king. Its defences were repaired and new temporary ramparts and palisades built, but when Ludlow was attacked by Colonel Birch's army in April 1646 the Royalist cause was already lost. Even so, many buildings outside the walls were destroyed by the defenders to improve lines of fire, and others were then burnt by the attackers. Fortunately, the siege only lasted a few weeks and few lives were lost before one of the last Royalist towns fell to the Parliament.

8 The fine mid-fifteenth-century roof of St Laurence's reflects the town's prosperity during the late medieval period and is the best in the county.

Ludlow continued to suffer during the Commonwealth and throughout the rest of the century. The Council of the Marches was revived after the Restoration, but was finally disbanded for good in 1689 and the town's long history as a regional capital ended. Ludlow was still in the doldrums in the early eighteenth century, and in 1722 Defoe called it 'a tolerable Place, but it decays to be sure with the rest . . . '. The remainder of the century saw a dramatic revival as Ludlow became a fashionable town with its own 'season'. Members of the local gentry built or rented fine Georgian houses in the principal streets, many of which survive. The eighteenth century also saw the first stirrings of a tourist industry. The romantic aspects of Ludlow's castle and the surrounding scenery made it a prime attraction to the rich aristocrats and others with time and money on, and in, their hands. In 1772 such a visitor, as well as being impressed with the 'abundance of pretty ladies' in the town, declared Ludlow to be 'one of the neatest, clean, pretty towns in England. The street by which you enter the town is spacious, with handsome houses, sash-windowed, on each side . . .'. In 1797 the *Gentleman's Magazine* called it 'one of the handsomest country towns in England'.

By 1800 Ludlow's population had grown to almost 4,000 and the town had a flourishing glove-making industry, several maltings, paper and corn mills, and the usual collection of small-scale industries associated with any sizeable market town. This did not satisfy one pamphleteer, who in 1810 accused the townspeople of being 'torpid with respect to improvements . . . wrapped up in your own little self-importance, and the enjoyments of domestic comfort'. He considered that coal and chemicals could be brought to Ludlow and artificial mineral baths established to create a spa town, complete with grand housing schemes south of the river – Whitcliff Crescent, Ludford Row and Charlton Place. Nothing happened and Ludlow never tried to rival Bath or Cheltenham.

The town was bypassed by the direct effects of the Industrial Revolution and, literally, by the canals of the late eighteenth century. The railway, in the guise of the Shrewsbury & Hereford, did not arrive until 1852. Nationally, the improvements in transport in the early Victorian period

effectively ended the rural 'season' in towns such as Ludlow. The gentry were able to travel further afield – to London, Bath, or the new seaside resorts. Ludlow continued, and continues, to be an important market town but one with limited industrial developments. It now has a population approaching 8,000 and has a thriving tourist trade. In June and July it hosts the famous Ludlow Festival with a variety of art events, capped by the open-air performances of Shakespeare against the dramatic backdrop of the castle.

Ludlow has a fine collection of Georgian doorcases of many different styles. Left to right: late Georgian doorcase in Corve Street; porch of High Hall, Castle Square, probably by T.F. Pritchard; doorway in Dinham with 'Gibbsian' surround; elegant, neo-classical Mill Street doorway with an ornate fanlight.

Architectural Character

Ludlow has retained its grid-iron medieval street pattern and has only really overflowed into the surrounding countryside in the last hundred years or so. Most of this later development has been to the east of the old town, with renewed development since the 1960s now approaching the bypass, opened in 1979. Unlike typical medieval streets, Ludlow's thoroughfares are surprisingly wide and spacious and show off the town's buildings to full advantage. The back lanes and the crowded east end of the old market-place provide a suitable contrast. Ludlow has far more than its fair share of historic buildings but, excepting the castle and church, it is not a town of splendid individual buildings. Instead, it is a town in which the quality of buildings as a whole is almost uniformly good; it is, above all, a town of memorable streetscapes.

The historic buildings have had to adapt through the centuries to the changing status and needs of their owners, and Ludlow's Georgian façades hide many medieval secrets. The oldest surviving buildings in Ludlow – the castle, church, town walls and remnants of larger medieval houses such as the Governor's Lodge and Barnaby House – are all built of stone. The overall impression of the rest of the town is, however, of timber frame and brick. This gives a very misleading impression on two counts. On the one hand, most buildings up to the late seventeenth century would, indeed, have been timber-framed and the majority have simply not survived. On the other, buildings continued to be built of stone right up until the nineteenth century and, in the Georgian period in particular, were simply

9 The rich architectural variety of the town is shown in this view eastwards along High Street towards the top of Broad Street. On the left are late sixteenth-century timber frames, one with Regency bow windows. Beyond them is the neo-classical mid-eighteenth century Butter Cross. To its right are more timber frames, a jettied medieval structure on the corner and, alongside, a Victorian façade to a much earlier fabric.

fronted in the more fashionable brick. The local stone, much of it quarried in Whitcliff, is a Silurian limestone and not a particularly good building stone. It can only really be used in rubble construction and is not easily worked up as ashlar – smooth-faced and squared stone.

The natural building material in a well-wooded country such as Shropshire was timber, and, in particular, English oak. Timber-framed buildings were normally pre-fabricated, with the pieces measured, sawn and temporarily slotted together on the floor of the carpenter's yard. Individual joints were then numbered, usually in Roman numerals, so that when the timbers were carted to the building site, the frames could be put back together in the same order. These carpenters' marks can often be seen scratched or gouged into the faces of the timbers.

10 Lower Broad Street was badly affected by the Civil War siege when both defenders and attackers destroyed buildings in the suburbs – for different reasons. The Georgian superstructure of the medieval Broad Gate has a magnificent Regency bay window. The once steep incline was lessened by Telford in the early nineteenth century by the creation of an embankment on this side of the gate, and a cutting on the other.

17

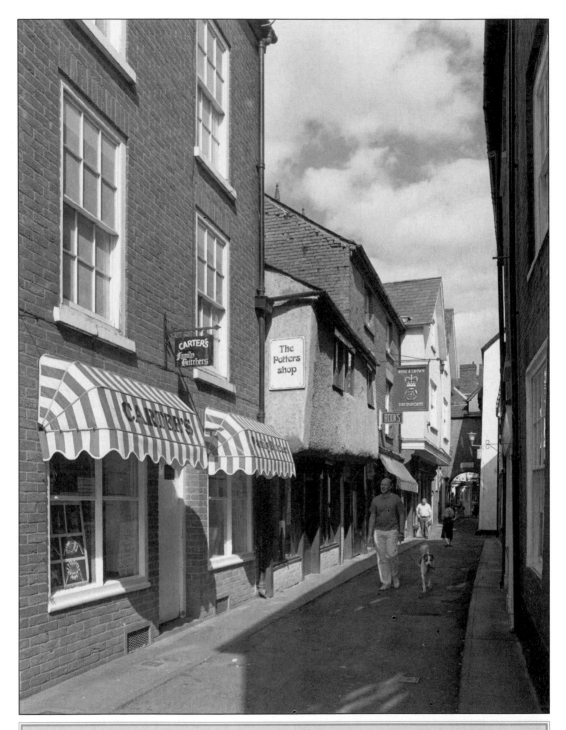

11 Temporary market stalls in the large medieval market-place on the crest of the hill, were gradually replaced by more substantial structures that eventually became proper buildings in their own right. This resulted in the formation of narrow alleyways, such as this one, Church Street, flanked by buildings of many different periods.

12 Tucked away behind Quality Square, off the market-place, is an intriguing relic of medieval Ludlow. This window probably dates to the late thirteenth or early fourteenth centuries but has been reset into its present position. Did it perhaps come from St Laurence's Church during the rebuilding work of the fifteenth century? Or was it from some grand merchant's house, lighting his Grand Hall or Solar?

13 Although the low-lying area near to the confluence of Teme and Corve known as the Linney was burgaged in the medieval period it does not seem to have been developed. Much later, fairly humble houses were built along a narrow street running below the northern town wall.

All the surviving timber-framed buildings in Ludlow are of box-frame construction, and often jettied. The jettying out of one or more of the upper floors on one or more sides is common. It was not, as is often thought, done to increase floor space, but helped to make the upper floors more stable because of the weight distribution of the jettied frames. Jetties tended to be quite wide in the medieval period, with overhangs often up to three feet or more, but they got shallower towards the end of the sixteenth century and became virtually decorative.

The panels in medieval timber framing were very large, and braces, usually curved, often had to be introduced into the framing to keep it rigid. As time wore on the size of the panels was reduced, until the decorative panels of Ludlow's fine collection of late sixteenth-century timber frames were quite small. The panels were infilled with wattle and daub. Staves were fitted into a series of drilled holes in the under-side of the upper rail of the

14 Ludlow has its own version of the more famous Rows of Chester. Timber-framed buildings at the top end of Broad Street encroached into the road and, eventually, an ad hoc arcade developed supported by cast-iron pillars. De Grey's Café is one of the town's renowned institutions.

panel and then sprung into a long groove on the top of the lower rail. Pliable branches were then woven between the staves to complete the key (the wattle) for the daub – an often horrendous mixture of dung, clay and animal hair. This was covered by a thin plaster skin.

Another type of framing that became popular, particularly in the sixteenth century, was close-studding. Vertical posts, or studs, in the frame were placed very close together, usually only the same distance as their width away from the next stud. It was a deliberately expensive use of timber and was usually only seen on the main fronts of buildings. A typical example of this is the Great House in Corve Street.

By the late sixteenth century the nation's timber reserves were dwindling and various laws were passed to conserve stocks and ensure sufficient timber for the navy. In Shropshire the richer merchants began to deliberately embellish their houses with plenty of ornately-carved timbers simply to show off their wealth. The Ludlow style is generally less ostentatious than that of Shrewsbury, but had its own particular features – including bold and very finely carved jetty brackets. The one building that outdid all others in the county for sheer ebullience is the world-famous Feathers in the Bull Ring.

Brick arrived late into Shropshire and was initially only used in chimneys. Timber framing or stone continued to be the main building materials in Ludlow until well into the eighteenth century. Indeed, no brick building in Ludlow seems to be definitely dated to before the 1710s, although, one or two may be slightly earlier and there was a reference in 1633 to a 'Brick House'. The belated arrival of brick radically changed the face of the town and, with few exceptions, was the only material considered good enough for the new Georgian houses. More often than not the old timber frames were simply given fashionable brick fronts, and when brick was too expensive, timber frames were plastered over and painted. The new fashion called for flat symmetrical façades, sash windows, and roofs hidden by parapets. The rich red bricks were all hand-made locally.

Not a great deal is known of the architects or craftsmen that worked in Ludlow. Until the eighteenth century most would have been local men, jobbing builders either following the local traditions or adapting them to the new styles slowly percolating

15 When timber frames were no longer in fashion, and fashion-conscious owners were not rich, the fronts of their houses could be plastered as a cheap way of trying to keep up with the times. This example is in Lower Broad Street.

16 Despite appearances there is a lot of stone building in Ludlow, but usually the stone is hidden and not used on the façades. This five-bay early eighteenth-century house in Corve Street has a brick front, now painted, but the side walls are of the local rubblestone.

This late eighteenth-century door surround in Corve Street has a rather unusual combination of decorative features taken from several different architectural styles, and the overall effect is rather heavy and cluttered.

through to the borders. The style of even the better houses can appear to be naïve, such as the overdone Venetian windows of No. 39 Broad Street or the heavy Gibbsian surrounds to the doors and windows of No. 11 Dinham, but this only adds to the town's charm. In the mid-eighteenth century William Baker, then based in Cheshire, designed the new Butter Cross as well as at least one house in Broad Street, later demolished. The Shrewsbury architect Thomas Farnolls Pritchard is known to have worked in the town. Better known for being involved in the famous Iron Bridge project, Pritchard was one of the county's most influential architects. Among his Ludlow contracts was the refronting of the medieval Guildhall in Mill Street with a very individual 'gothick' brick façade complete with elaborate doorcase to match.

Georgian restraint continued in Ludlow well into the nineteenth century, and the centre of the town has few flamboyant

17 No. 37 Broad Street is a fine example of the symmetry and elegance of the new Georgian houses being built in Ludlow throughout the eighteenth century. The glazing bars are mercifully complete in the shallowly recessed sashes and it is interesting to see how, to save money, the top floor windows were given casements. The brick quoins and the lack of a parapet to hide the roof are slightly unusual for a mid-eighteenth century date.

What not to do with a Georgian doorway. The heavy gothick fanlight doesn't match the simplicity of the neo-classical pilasters anyway, but the door design is a modern disaster and completely out of character. Otherwise, this house in Broad Street has been fairly well cared for.

Victorian buildings. The neo-everything work of the nineteenth century can be very striking and attractive in its own right, but is out of place in the gentle elegance of a town like Ludlow. Here it is not even the style that jars the senses: generally it is what the buildings are built of. The new railways brought in glazed bricks of varied colours and polished stone from many parts, all clashing with the mellow local materials. Fortunately, there are very few discordant buildings – though whether this was because of the town's lack of industrial growth or because of innate good taste is a moot point.

Unlike in other historic western midland towns such as Shrewsbury and Chester, there were few attempts at grandiose

Victorian mock timber frames with their inaccurate magpie colour schemes and overblown details. The new interest in old buildings towards the end of the century did, however, result in the lath-and-plaster skims, once added to hide old-fashioned timbers, being stripped away and the frames exposed again to the elements – and admiration. The top end of Broad Street, for example, was completely altered by this process in the early years of this century.

As the twentieth century progressed the town's strong civic identity helped to save many threatened historic buildings. Perhaps the key campaign was that to save the old Tolsey in the Bull Ring, destined for demolition in 1956 as part of a road widening scheme. As well as preserving its old buildings, Ludlow has escaped the excesses of modern architecture, and its modern buildings are no better or no worse than they should be. Great efforts have been made in the centre of the town to ensure that new buildings harmonize with the old and do not detract from them. This is, of course, very laudable, and Ludlow has succeeded where too many similar towns have failed. Generally the scale and the materials of new building has been well chosen; it is just a pity that the details – of the doors and windows, for example – do not have a more positive contribution to make to the town's architecture. There is always the danger of buildings built to be discrete becoming bland and boring.

But these are minor niggles, the sort made to an old and much-loved friend. Today's planners, and a very active Civic Society, are helping to make sure that Ludlow's unique architectural heritage is preserved for future generations while also ensuring that this busy market town does not fossilize into a characterless tourist trap.

The Castle and Defences

The Saxons built no castles and failed to realize their military importance. The Normans, on the other hand, used the castle as their main weapon in subduing England and, later, Wales. Most of the early Norman castles were swiftly constructed motte-and-baileys, generally built of earth and timber; Ludlow was a rare exception, built in stone. The original castle is now the Inner Bailey and was sited on the cliffs overlooking the river. A rock-cut defensive ditch guarded the easier approach from the south and east, and provided a convenient quarry for the walls.

The castle consisted of a fairly low curtain wall, a simple gate-house, and several open-backed mural towers. Inside these walls would have been a variety of timber-framed buildings, some probably connected with the open-backed towers. The north-western tower has a complicated system of mural passages and vices – stone spiral staircases – that also give access to two very fine garderobes – or toilets. It is possible that the tower was connected with an important domestic building, possibly the private quarters of the owner or the great hall itself. The original gate-house was soon raised into a gatehouse-keep, a rare structure but one also found at a similar site at Richmond Castle, Yorkshire. The famous round Norman chapel inside the castle was also a later addition to the original work.

By the end of the twelfth century the castle was considerably extended by the creation of a large Outer Bailey and a similar feature can be found at another de Lacy stronghold, Trim Castle near Dublin. The Outer Bailey and its new gateway facing the High Street made the old gatehouse-keep redundant. Its archway

was filled in and a new gateway pierced the curtain wall along-side it. The blocking of the first gateway and the rough stonework that supported the original drawbridge can still be seen.

The next major changes occurred a century later after the castle came into the hands of the de Genevilles. It was probably Peter de Geneville who started building a magnificent first-floor hall and a Solar Block against the inside of the northern curtain wall. The design was changed at least once during building, but then work seems to have stopped before it was finished, possibly as a result of Peter's fairly early death. The work may have been completed by Roger de Mortimer, who certainly added a matching wing of domestic apartments at the opposite end of the Great Hall from the Solar Block. The result was a magnificent palace suitable for a man of Mortimer's regal pretensions. He is also

18 The Great Hall range of the castle was probably started in the thirteenth century and finished by the notorious Roger de Mortimer in the early fourteenth, just before his downfall. The hall itself is to the left, and was approached by stone steps. Its central window was blocked when a more convenient wall fireplace replaced the open hearth in Tudor times.

19 Virtually hidden beneath a Georgian house, itself remodelled several times before the Regency, is the former Broad Gate. Its defensive capabilities are more obvious from the outside. The Georgian buildings to the right probably date to the 1720s.

credited with building St Peter's Chapel in the Outer Bailey in thanks for his safe return from exile.

More changes followed in the late fifteenth century when the north wall of the old keep, or great tower, was rebuilt and new floors added inside the structure. Further alterations followed in the next century when the Council of the Marches used it as their headquarters. Great changes were made in the Great Hall range in the Inner Bailey, and new stables and lodgings were added to the Outer Bailey. The most impressive new building was the Judges' Lodging, completed in 1581 and a fine example of a late Tudor domestic building. This was built at the expense of Sir Henry Sidney, the then Lord President, whose arms can be found above the gateway nearby. In 1618 the Earl of Northampton ordered 'a house for riding' to be built at the castle, part of an ambitious 'Academy for the instruction of young gentlemen in

horsemanship' – but virtually nothing is known of what became of the scheme.

No real changes seem to have been made to the castle to defend it against the Parliament during the Civil War, although the insertion of gunports into some of the battlements may date from this period. The castle was, surprisingly, not slighted after it fell in 1646 and was reoccupied by the restored Council after the Restoration. Once the Council was finally disbanded in 1689, the castle quickly began to fall into dereliction. Although still containing an 'abundance of coats of arms . . . together with lances, spears, firelocks and old armour' when William Stukeley visited in 1721, he lamented that 'the present inhabitants live upon the sale of the timber, stone, iron, and other materials and furniture, which dwindle away insensibly'. Defoe, a year later, described the castle as being 'in the very Perfection of Decay'.

20 Ludlow Castle was one of a very few Norman castles to be built in stone from the beginning. The keep is generally considered one of the most complicated Norman structures in the country. It seems to have started off as a fairly small gatehouse that was then raised and later radically remodelled. The tower to the left is also Norman, while the gable to the right over the later gateway belongs to the Judges Lodging of 1581.

20 Parts of the original curtain wall contain dark and gloomy mural passages. This one, leading off the north-west tower, is one of a pair of stepped passages that led, via spiral staircases, to garderobes and upper passageways.

21 A great deal of the late thirteenth-century town wall survives, though much of it is tucked away in private gardens and most of it has been repaired many times over the past 600 years. This stretch is between Broad Street and Old Street. Originally, the area now occupied by lawn and flower-beds would have been a deep ditch.

22 The late thirteenth-century Broad Gate, with its flanking towers, portcullis, and well-guarded passageway would have presented a formidable obstacle to any attackers. The abutments of the drawbridge survive in the cellar of the adjacent building.

23 Parts of Old Street Gate, which appears to have been fairly similar to the Broad Gate, survived until the early nineteenth century, and some masonry may survive in this much altered late medieval building built on to the former town wall. Shortly after 1676 this became part of the workhouse and, in 1837, part of Lane's Asylum – actually almshouses.

The castle was still a royal possession and in 1771 the government wanted to demolish it and sell off the reusable building materials. They commissioned T.F. Pritchard to see whether the idea was feasible, and he seems to have deliberately undervalued the potential value of the material, and overrated the costs of demolition, and so saved the castle from certain destruction. Inevitably, the old timbers and floors rotted away, but at least the bulk of the masonry survived; Pritchard really does deserve his own blue plaque! In the same year the Earl of Powis leased the site, and his widow laid out walks around it along the line of the former outer ditch and on the precipitous slopes down to the river. Another Earl finally purchased the castle in 1811 and it has remained in the family's hands ever since. In the 1980s a new programme of renovation and repair began that is still continuing.

In the thirteenth century Shropshire was troubled by sporadic Welsh uprisings. In 1233 Ludlow was granted permission

24 The Linney Gate was little more than a postern gate providing a short cut through to the Linney meadows from the churchyard. This rather out-of-place polychrome brick affair is a Victorian shell of 1888 built to protect its fragmentary remains.

to build a town wall, but in 1294 this was described as 'broken down and decayed'. A new grant of murage – that is, the right to levy tolls on goods entering the town to pay for the upkeep of the walls – was issued. Most of the surviving walls, although much patched and repaired, probably belong to this period. The walls did not protect the whole town, and the lower parts of the three main southern streets were outside them. Corve Street was also left outside the main defensive wall but did have an additional gate near the base of the hill, known as the Lower Corve Gate. In front of the walls was a wide ditch except, presumably, on the much steeper slopes on the north and west side of the town. The best surviving stretch of the wall is that on St John's Road, between the Broad Street Gate and the site of the Old Street Gate, where remnants of a later medieval building survive. Flower-beds and lawns now occupy the site of the ditch. Another good section survives behind houses in the Linney.

Although Leland claimed there were just five gates there appear to have been seven. All these gates, bar the Broad Street Gate, were demolished by the end of the eighteenth century to improve traffic circulation. The Broad Street Gate, guarding the entrance from Ludford Bridge, was clearly the most important entrance to the town. Even now, partially encased within a large Georgian house, it is impressive. In style it is typical of the Edwardian period of castle building and defences, with two round towers flanking the gate-passage. The supports for the drawbridge over the ditch survive in the cellars of the nearby pub. Anyone who got as far as the entrance would have been confronted by the portcullis and been subject to withering fire from the defenders through loops on either side that are now blocked up. The main danger to pedestrians today is from the cars carefully negotiating the narrow medieval gate-passage.

Churches

The 135-foot high tower of St Laurence's dominates the surrounding south Shropshire countryside, a symbol of the town's medieval wealth. Older towns, such as Shrewsbury and Hereford, often had several parishes and money tended to be shared around the individual parish churches. Ludlow had a single new parish and all the available wealth could be lavished on the one church. This is why it could be virtually rebuilt in the middle of the fifteenth century and become the largest parish church in the county. There is no mention of the church until 1199 when it was being enlarged. As it lies on the crest of the hill just to the north of High Street, and was originally in its own grid-square in the planned settlement, it was probably founded in the mid-twelfth century. Once dedicated to three saints, St Philip and St James were quietly 'dropped' by the end of the fourteenth century.

Only fragments survive of the early church, and not a great deal remains of the thirteenth-century work apart from the fine Early English south doorway. That door is approached through one of only two hexagonal porches in the country, built in the early–mid-fourteenth century in the second broad development of English Gothic – the Decorated. The only other porch of this type is the contemporary north porch of St Mary's, Redcliffe, in Bristol; no doubt there were trading links between the two towns but no one really knows which porch came first. The fine north aisle, with its beautiful windows, stained glass, and rich ball-flower decoration, dates to the start of the century, and was built by the de Verdon family of Alton, Staffordshire, who held part of the manor.

Both transepts were also rebuilt in the fourteenth century but, despite this, the general feeling of the church, inside and out, is definitely Perpendicular – the final true phase of English Gothic. The crowning glory of the church is the crossing tower, which was under construction in 1469 when several consultants

were brought in from other areas to advise on the work. At this time Ludlow was enjoying the patronage of the recently victorious Edward IV. The radical rebuilding in the middle decades of the fifteenth century was largely financed by the powerful Palmers' Gild. The stained glass in their own guild chapel in the church tells of the legend of their foundation by Edward the Confessor. Other local guilds also had chapels in the church, including the Fletchers'. From the late fifteenth century onwards, the church was left virtually unaltered, apart from internal fixtures and fittings, for nearly four centuries. It was then worked on, at two different stages, by two of the best-known Victorian ecclesiastical architects, Sir George Gilbert Scott and Sir Arthur Blomfield.

The internal alterations cleared away later additions from the nave and chancel. The interior now rivals that of any parish

25 The magnificent interior of St Laurence's Church rivals that of many cathedrals. Although the church incorporates the fabric of earlier phases, its character is almost entirely the Perpendicular of the mid-fifteenth century. Much of the cost of church and fittings was paid for by the Palmers' Gild.

26 There are only two hexagonal church porches in Britain, one to the south door of St Laurence's and the other at St Mary Redcliffe in Bristol. Both date to the early fourteenth century though it is not at all clear which one was built first. The difference between old and replacement stone is striking.

27 St Laurence's is one of the finest parish churches in the Midlands and the largest in Shropshire. Its tower was built around 1469 but heavily restored in the last century. The aisle in the foreground was built in the early fourteenth century.

church in the country and is almost cathedral-like in its scale. In the nave are the fine stalls and misericords, restored but mostly dating to the fifteenth century. The misericords were lift-up seats with a special corbel on which the occupant could rest his back-side during the interminable medieval services – while still looking like he was standing up. They were often carved with great vigour, and humour, and St Laurence's has the best set in the region. The church also boasts a carillon of eight bells, playing tunes on the hour.

St Laurence's may be the largest church in the town but it is certainly not the oldest. That particular honour goes to the chapel

27 St Laurence's famous set of misericords mostly dates from the late 1440s and was probably paid for by the Palmers' Gild. Some commemorate powerful men such as the king and the Duke of York, and others are morality tales in wood. The rich variety of the subject matter and the obvious sense of fun and satire of some of them offers an otherwise unobtainable insight into the character of a lost age.

At a time when there were rumblings of discontent between the Houses of York and Lancaster, whoever carved the misericords was careful not to upset either party. The falcon and fetterlock was the personal emblem of Richard, Duke of York, the father of Edward IV and manorial Lord of Ludlow.

The man with the impish grin pulling up his hose may well have been modelled on someone that the craftsman knew. He is carrying a large load, probably of cloth or fleeces, so could be connected with the local woollen industry.

The seductive mermaid in this carving probably once had a comb for her tangled tresses in her left hand and still has a mirror in the other. A medieval equivalent to a Page Three girl, and just as sexist, she is a warning against the sin of lust. Her fierce-looking attendants may be dolphins, but could be fish – symbol of the human soul and thus in her thrall.

Drunkenness was another sin, according to the Church, but although this scene is meant, presumably, to show its evils, the tipsy chap seems to be enjoying himself. He is filling a jug from a barrel of ale or mead, but seems scarcely capable of standing up straight.

The gorged antelope was the emblem of the Lancastrian Henry VI; the flanking 'Green Men', ancient fertility symbols, are rather odd companions.

The crowned king depicted on this misericord is less obviously identifiable. He has been considered to be Edward III, the last undisputed king of the royal line who died in 1377.

The slightly different headgear of this woman clearly called for some comment, and the two lads on either side appear to be poking fun at her. It is a warning against the evils of vanity, though whether it depicts a real person or a then well-known character from a medieval mystery play is less certain.

Another well-known mythological figure of the time was the griffin – half eagle, half lion. The quality of the carving is exquisite and it is difficult to believe that it was done well over 500 years ago.

of St Mary Magdalene in the Inner Bailey of the castle, which probably dates to the early–mid-eleventh century – and is a real gem of Norman architecture. It is almost unique, having a completely round nave, a feature usually attributed to the influence of the Knights Templar. The west door and chancel arch both show off rich decoration typical of the period, and inside is a bench and arcade running around the wall. The original chancel and polygonal apse were pulled down in the sixteenth century and replaced by a longer and plainer chancel that has in turn disappeared. At the same time a first floor was inserted linked by a two-storey corridor to the adjacent Great Hall range, allowing the 'haves' to worship in the same chapel as the 'have nots' without being seen. Also in the castle grounds are the more fragmentary remains of Roger Mortimer's St Peter's Chapel, built in 1328 to celebrate his safe return from exile and his rise to total

28 There are only a handful of round chapels in Britain. St Mary Magdalene's in the castle dates from the first half of the twelfth century and has some fine Norman carving. Its original chancel was replaced in the sixteenth century, and its replacement has also been demolished.

power. His hypocritical piety was wasted and the chapel was later used as a court room.

Just outside the castle walls in Dinham are the remains of another chapel, recently restored and partially incorporated into a house. The chapel was dedicated to St Thomas the Martyr – Thomas à-Becket, the Archbishop of Canterbury murdered in his own cathedral in 1170 and canonized three years later. The style of the surviving features, including the round-headed doorways and the plain quadripartite ribbed vault, suggests a date soon after Thomas's death. The chapel is thus the oldest building in the town outside the castle walls, and was probably built on the site of an older one. It had become derelict by the mid-sixteenth century and was subsequently adapted much later for secular purposes; at the start of the twentieth century it was a furniture warehouse. There is an older church still, but not in Ludlow town. Over the river in Ludford, St Giles's Church, next to Ludford house, has a Norman nave. The chancel was built in the late thirteenth century but its finest work is the Fox Chapel, added in the 1550s.

29 The interior of St Thomas's Chapel in Dinham.

30 Hidden away in Ludford is St Giles's Church, which is well worth finding. Parts of it are Norman, and it has a fine sixteenth-century private chapel built by the Fox family. Note the small window in the end wall of the nave that would have lit the rood-loft, a common feature of churches before the Reformation.

Two other chapels deserve mention, although both have long-since been demolished. St Leonard's, in Corve Street, was founded in the twelfth century and taken down in the eighteenth, but a late twelfth-century tympanum has recently been discovered in the masonry of a nearby house. A small chapel, St Catherine's, was built, certainly before the start of the fifteenth century, on a cutwater of Ludford Bridge. A similar chapel survives on a bridge at St Ives, Cambridgeshire. The Ludlow chapel survived well into the eighteenth century before being taken down.

Ludlow had two friaries. The friars' preachers considered that the old monastic orders had lost their spiritual way and were no longer spreading the Word. Various new orders of travelling preachers developed in the early thirteenth century dedicated to poverty and preaching. By 1254 the Austin Friars (or Augustinians) had occupied temporary quarters in Dinham, but within two years had moved to a new site just outside the town in Lower Galdeford. Nearly a century later, in 1350, a Carmelite house was established at the bottom end of Corve Street next to the twelfth-century chapel of St Leonard's. Both friaries were closed in 1538 and their buildings eventually demolished. The Carmelite site was then rented by Thomas Vernon, who handed in to the Council of the Marches the friaries' valuables, found hidden in 'an old hose' in a ditch nearby. These consisted of just 'two cruets and a pax of silver, two chalices, one patent, and the foot of a monstrall [sic] . . . '. Part of this site was excavated in the 1980s and the footings exposed. Sadly the excellent display panels have now been removed, presumably because of vandalism, and the site is wildly overgrown.

Older than both friaries, another conventual house was the Hospital of St John the Baptist at the bottom end of Broad Street near to the Ludford Bridge. It was founded in the early thirteenth century to care for the sick or the poverty-stricken but, as with most similar houses, became more a quasi-religious, and rather corrupt, establishment. There were just two brethren left at the Dissolution. Fragments of the rubble-built Hospital, including a heavily restored two-centred archway, can still be seen. Equally fragmentary, and generally less accessible, are the remains of the college founded at the end of the fourteenth century by the

31 St John's Hospital was founded in the thirteenth century near to Ludford Bridge and at the bottom of Lower Broad Street. A casualty of the Dissolution, sections of it later became part of the Bell Inn. It is now difficult to tell how much of the present masonry is original.

32 Redundant buildings have always posed a problem for conservationists. Demolition is a brutal, but obvious, answer but many are capable of taking on a new lease of life. 'Adaptive re-use' were architectural buzz-words of the 1980s and many sympathetic schemes were developed. The reuse of the former Old Street Primitive Methodist chapel (built in 1871) is not one of them.

33 It is quite rare in small towns to find a masonic hall so boldly announced by its regalia. This nineteenth-century structure is on Brand Lane, the narrow lane linking the three main streets of the town. Architecturally it is very amateurish; its classical motifs are poorly thought out, and there is no sense of form or proportion.

Palmers' Gild off College Street near the church to house their chaplains. John Leland, in about 1540, described it as 'a fayr hows at the west end of the paroche church yard'. Alongside, the Gild supported an almshouse.

No significant contributions were made to the ecclesiastic architecture of Ludlow for almost four centuries after the completion of St Laurence's. Even then, none of the nineteenth-century work calls for much comment. Two new Church of England chapels were built in the standard, neo-Gothic style. In 1871 a new St Leonard's was built in Corve Street as a chapel of ease for the nearby Foxe's Almshouses; it also served the

34 St Leonard's Chapel in Corve Street was built in 1871 on land next to the former Carmelite friary that had become a graveyard. An earlier St Leonard's, of Norman date, was demolished in the late eighteenth century. Recently the Victorian chapel was declared redundant, and it is now an antiques centre.

35 The former Methodist chapel off Lower Broad Street was opened in 1800. It is typically humble – but later nonconformist chapels tended to become almost as ornate as mainstream Church of England buildings. The chapel is now a private house.

cemetery. Now redundant, it has been converted into an antiques centre. St John's Chapel in Gravel Hill, of 1881, is of little note, despite being designed by Sir Arthur Blomfield – one of the better architects working in the region. Nonconformity was always fairly strong in Ludlow but none of the surviving chapels are of great architectural interest. The oldest surviving example, the Methodist chapel built in 1800 in an alley off Lower Broad Street, is now a private house. Dominating the eastern suburbs of Ludlow is the domed Byzantine-revival Roman Catholic Church of St Peter's, in Henley Road, designed by a G. Rinvolucci in 1936.

Public Buildings

For a town of its size and importance, and one that was for so long the administrative capital of a large area, Ludlow has surprisingly few public buildings of note. True, much of the work of the Council of the Marches took place within the castle itself in buildings built or adapted for the purpose, and several other buildings, such as Pritchard's Gaol in Tower Street and the former theatre in Mill Street, have been pulled down.

Nevertheless, there are not many towns of Ludlow's size that do not even boast a town hall! The last town hall also served as the market hall and stood in Castle Square; it was the one major Victorian building the town possessed and was started in 1888 – despite its date plaque of 1887, Queen Victoria's Jubilee. The result of an architectural competition, it was built of fiery red brick, rather ill-proportioned, and certainly over-decorated. As early as 1913 it was considered 'somewhat out of character with its surroundings'. Later writers have been more forthright. Pevsner called it 'Ludlow's bad luck' and Alec Clifton-Taylor, a 'detestable building'. It was declared unsafe in 1986 and pulled down almost straight away – leaving once again a large and open market-place.

For many years, the functions of a town hall were carried out on the upper floor of the oddly named Butter Cross at the top of Broad Street. This ashlar-faced building was designed by William Baker, finished in 1744, and now dominates the famous view up the street. As an example of classical architecture it is rather amateurish – a combination of provincial Palladianism with a hint of the older Baroque – but it has a certain honesty

36 William Baker's Butter Cross, at the top of Broad Street, was finished in 1744, but the extension to the left has spoilt the symmetry of the composition. The style is certainly not pure, but it has presence and suits its dominant position in the streetscape. The bell in the wooden cupola is said to have come from old St Leonard's Chapel in Corve Street.

37 Lane's House is a rather rambling affair of different dates and materials, built just inside the former Old Street Gate. It seems to have been rebuilt in the early seventeenth century, but the initials 'E.G.' in the left-hand dormer have been added later. After 1676, together with the medieval building to the left, built on the site of the gatehouse, it was taken over by the trustees of Thomas Lane and used as the workhouse. In 1837 they became almshouses, and were renamed Lane's Asylum. The modern change of name is perhaps understandable.

about it and contrasts well with the recently exposed timber frames nearby. Its open ground floor is still used for various sales during the year.

Not far from the Butter Cross, in the Bull Ring, is a much older building with market connections – the Tolsey. The Bull Ring does not get its name from the barbarous 'sport' of bull-baiting, but because this end of the medieval market was reserved for the beast market. As its name suggests, the Tolsey was the building where the tolls from the market were collected and its upper floor was also the place from which the market was administered and where disputes were settled. The timber-framed building has been heavily restored several times and is difficult to date accurately. Judging from the large size of its panels it is probably late medieval, perhaps of the fifteenth century. It remained in use until the late seventeenth century

38 This row of two-storey stone houses in Corve Street could have been built any time in the seventeenth or even early eighteenth century but dates to 1590. They are known as Foxe's Almshouses, being the gift of Charles Foxe and built near the site of the demolished Carmelite friary.

39 The medieval Tolsey, in the Bull Ring, was the building from which the market was administered – tolls were taken and a small court dealt with any disputes. For many years it was covered with lath and plaster and was threatened with demolition in the 1950s. Saved by public pressure, it was renovated in 1962, when its timbers were exposed.

40 The building now used by the local library, in Old Street, has a Regency façade, a rarity in Ludlow, and boasts a lovely pair of bow windows. This front was added when the building was an important hostelry, the Golden Lion.

when it became a house and shop. It was restored at the start of the present century and was then threatened with demolition in the 1950s to make way for road improvements. Thankfully it was saved and, shortly afterwards, restored again and its timber framing exposed to view.

The influential Palmers' Gild had a guildhall on the site of the present Guildhall in Mill Street as early as the thirteenth century. Behind T.F. Pritchard's rococo gothick brick façade of 1768, with its pointed arches, classical symmetry, and elaborate porch, are the substantial remains of a medieval hall possibly of fifteenth-century date. Across, and slightly lower down the street is another large hall of similar date that also belonged to the Gild. The Palmers' Hall of Ludlow College was originally built as part of a rich merchant's house. The Gild had established a school near St Laurence's in the early fifteenth century that

41 The Palmers' Hall of Ludlow College is near the bottom of Mill Street. The college was formerly the grammar school, one of the oldest in the country and founded by the Palmers' Gild. The school moved to this site in 1527, taking over the medieval hall house built by a rich wool merchant. The largest arched doorway would have led to the screens passage, with the hall being on the left and the services to the right. The roof was raised to give additional accommodation for the school.

42 The Palmers' Gild had built a college for their chantry priests at the end of the fourteenth century not far from St Laurence's Church. The college, and the almshouses alongside, were then taken over by the borough. Much later, the local hospital occupied most of the site. In the last few years new sheltered housing, the modern equivalent of the almshouses, has been built. College Court's detailing may be a little mechanical but it has human scale and a sense of communal security and quiet.

moved to this site in 1527. When the Gild's affairs were taken over by the borough in 1551 the school came under its control and, although much altered, is still used for educational purposes.

The present college site also incorporates another medieval building that must, until recently, have been the oldest gymnasiums in the country. Barnaby House has a complex history but appears to have been built around 1300 as a narrow, two-storey structure possibly divided into small apartments. It is possible that there may be some truth in the tradition that it was built as a pilgrims' hostel. By the fifteenth century it had been converted into a house, owned by Thomas Barnaby, an official of the Duke

44 Another medieval building taken over by the former grammar school was Barnaby House. It has had an extremely chequered history since about 1300 and, traditionally, was built as a pilgrims' hostel. It later became the town house of an important Yorkist official, Thomas Barnaby, but then fell on hard times and was converted into cottages. At the start of this century it became the school's gymnasium and was recently converted into high-tech classrooms.

45 The Assembly Rooms on the corner of Castle Square and Mill Street were built by public subscription and opened in 1840. Designed by a local architect, Samuel Stead, the complex had a simple elegance that has been destroyed on the Castle Square frontage by those hideous ground-floor openings and an unsympathetic sign. It should only take a little thought to restore this useful public amenity to its former glory. Could this complex not take on many of the functions of the late Town Hall?

of York; its fine roof appears to date from this period but is actually re-used. It is feasible that it was brought from another building nearby – possibly one damaged when the Lancastrians took the town. By the seventeenth century the building was in decline and it was converted into cottages. Finally bought by the grammar school in the nineteenth century, the first floor was removed at the start of the twentieth when it became the school gym. In 1991 the floor was replaced and the building is now used as class-rooms. The High Hall of the college, in Castle Square and formerly part of the Girls' High School, was adapted from a grand eighteenth-century building.

One of Ludlow's finest nineteenth-century buildings has been ruined by twentieth-century alterations. The Assembly Rooms on the corner of Castle Square and Mill Street were built at a cost of just under £6,000 as the Public Rooms in 1840 to combine several different functions. Designed by local architect

46 Ludford Bridge used to link Shropshire, on the right, with Herefordshire, on the left. Rebuilt and repaired many times, it dates back in its present form to at least the fifteenth century and parts of it are probably older still. Like several medieval bridges, it once had its own chapel that catered for travellers and pilgrims.

Samuel Stead they included an assembly room, natural history museum, supper room, billiard room and a reading room. The building had a chaste neo-classical simplicity but all has been ruined by the insertion of two segmental-headed openings facing Castle Square that leave the first floor pilasters apparently supported by fresh air. The whole ensemble is in need of a coat of paint; it is a shame that this prominent and well-used building has not been treated with a little more respect over the years. A local group is now trying to raise funds to restore it properly.

Ludlow's three bridges, two over the Teme and one over the Corve, have always been very important, though it is not at all clear which bridge came first. It has been considered that the line of Old Street and Corve Street represents an ancient trackway that pre-dates Ludlow, which would suggest an early crossing point near Ludford downstream of the present one. Ludford

47 The graceful arches of Dinham Bridge were designed by John Straphen of Shrewsbury, and were finished in 1823. At low water the piers of the old bridge can be seen just downstream. Behind, the towers of the castle can be glimpsed through the trees.

Bridge in its present form probably dates to the late fifteenth century when it was rebuilt after partial demolition by the retreating Yorkist army in 1461.

The elegant Dinham Bridge was built in 1823 and, until the 1880s, was known as the New Bridge. It replaced a rather patched affair of brick and stone, that had, in the eighteenth century, been a rebuilding of a timber-arched bridge on stone piers. The piers may be very old indeed, and there could have been a bridge at this point, below the castle, soon after the town was founded. When the river is low, the piers of the old bridge can be seen just downstream of the new. At the other end of the town, Corve Bridge is of similar style to Dinham, but was apparently built in 1787, using some of the masonry from the old St Leonard's Chapel nearby in its foundations.

Ludlow has a delightful collection of windows of all shapes and sizes. Left to right: 'gothick' window belonging to the Wheatsheaf Inn near the Broadgate; Georgian window from a house in Broad Street; casement from a timber-framed house in Dinham; Georgian window from a house in Dinham.

Houses

One fine characteristic of Ludlow, all too rare in towns that expanded rapidly in the nineteenth century, is the fact that it is very much a lived-in town. For the most part the houses in the centre, even those lining the busiest streets, are still homes and have not all been converted into offices or store-rooms. This domesticity gives the town a special warmth and friendliness, and has also played an important part in protecting the town's architecture. Houses that are lived in tend to be looked after much better than those that have been converted to other uses – and are less likely to be subjected to unsympathetic changes. A town centre that is lived in is also generally better kept and less likely to suffer from neglect and vandalism.

No particularly early houses appear to have survived, the oldest ones probably dating only to the fourteenth century. Even these have been subject to many changes over the centuries and their original layouts are often difficult to detect. The traditional high status medieval house would have consisted of a large hall, usually single storey and open to the roof, with flanking two-storey wings of services and private quarters. When it was finished in the early fourteenth century, the magnificent Great Hall range in the castle shows this basic concept at its most splendid.

There were many variations of the basic theme, especially in towns where the layout usually had to be adapted to urban needs and the restricted size of urban burgage plots. It is perhaps strange, therefore, that the most obvious survival of a medieval hall house, the Palmers' Hall of the college in Mill Street already referred to, was built along the street and must have been a house of some note. Built of stone it was owned at one time by the Cheneys of Cheney Longville, a village near Craven Arms. Its arched doorway probably led to the cross (or screens) passage running across the bottom (or 'low') end of the hall between it and the service range.

The hall itself was heated by an open hearth, the billowing smoke finding its way, eventually, out through a louvre in the roof. At the 'high' end of the hall there would be a doorway leading to the owner's private quarters, usually termed the solar.

Several other open halls have been recognized by recent research in Ludlow, particularly by very active Ludlow Historical Research Group who identified four in Broad Street. Gradually the smoky open-hearths went out of fashion and the chimney allowed far more freedom in the layout of houses. Parlours, withdrawing rooms and bedchambers became the more important living rooms, leaving the much diminished halls for formal use or reduced them to little more than entrance lobbies. Privacy became more important than communal living, and the basic internal arrangement of houses by the end of the sixteenth century was little different from those of our own time.

(text continues on p. 72)

48 Behind a fairly bland late Georgian brick front on the Bull Ring lies the yard of the Bull Inn. The various timber frames range in date from the late medieval to the early seventeenth century – the oldest range being the jettied one to the right with its typically large panels.

49 This pair of typically tall, narrow, and ornate timber-framed buildings in High Street probably date to the late sixteenth century, but the splendid bow window on the house on the right was probably added in the Regency period. Both houses have been restored.

50 The row of tall chimneys in the long stone range by the main road in Ludford belong to the service range of Ludford House, probably built in the late sixteenth century. The road originally went around the east side of Ludford but was diverted to its present line in the early nineteenth century.

50 Ludford House, part of which is seen here through the porch of St Giles's Church, is a fine rambling pile of many periods built around a courtyard. Built of both masonry and timber framing, it dates mainly from the sixteenth to nineteenth centuries. This bay window is probably part of a Jacobean remodelling.

51 College Street, leading from the back of the Butter Cross past the churchyard to the site of the Linney Gate, only got its name officially in the 1880s. The rectory, the gabled building in the foreground, is much older and may have the oldest medieval roof in the town – possibly dating to the fourteenth century or before.

52 The Corner Shop, on the junction of Broad and King Streets, is a large medieval timber-framed building jettied on two sides and has typically large medieval panels. It also has a crown post roof, running back from the right-hand gable – one of only two identified so far in the town, the other being at No. 4 Broad Street. This type of roof in this area gradually fell out of favour after the fourteenth century. Its appearance was greatly improved in 1983 when black paint was stripped from its timber framing.

53 The Great House in Corve Street is officially dated to the early to mid-sixteenth century but could be slightly earlier. Owned by wealthy cloth manufacturers, and later by equally wealthy tanners, it eventually fell into decline. By the 1970s it was in such a poor state that it was bought by the local District Council, and restored in 1977–8 at great expense.

Architecturally, the surviving Ludlow houses indicate a fairly uniform local style, particularly by the end of the sixteenth century, that differed from larger towns nearby such as Shrewsbury and Worcester. There appear to be two main types of design, possibly reflecting two teams of craftsmen and builders. A common feature is a shallow jetty, supported by richly carved brackets, often with human figures on them. The first style is concerned with symmetry and proportion, using fairly loose close-studding on buildings of two storeys with very tall dormer-lit attics – York House in Corve Street being typical. The other is a more ornate style, generally of three

(text continues on p. 79)

54 Just a little further down Corve Street is a house very similar in style and date to the Great House, but here the differences in side and front framing are obvious. The wide jetty at the front has been underbuilt in brick.

55 York House, at the north end of Corve Street, lacks the ornate panelling of contemporary late sixteenth -century buildings but its well-balanced façade is elegant and sophisticated. The building was recently restored with help from a town-scheme grant. The timbers have, happily, not been blackened after the plaster cladding was removed, but allowed to retain their natural colour and patina.

56 By the second half of the sixteenth century a definite Ludlow style had evolved for the timber-framed houses of the wealthy merchants, and they were not only built on the main streets of the town. This fine example is on Raven Lane, the service alley between Broad and Mill Streets and is now two houses – Nos 14 and 15. The rather buxom lady carved into the top central bracket looks suspiciously modern!

57 Virtually next door to Nos 14 and 15 Raven Lane is another house clearly of the same period and probably of the same ornate timber framing. It has been derelict and forlorn for some time and is just waiting for someone to come along and restore it – and to rip off that hideous matchboarding.

58 Even in Ludlow historic buildings are still threatened by neglect and dereliction, as shown by this small late- sixteenth century building on Bell Lane. At some time in its history most of its wattle and daub panel infills have been replaced with brick – called brick-nogging – and its first-floor jetty has been underbuilt. Note the original windows, still with their mullions.

59 In the Georgian period many timber frames were hidden behind lath and plaster and made to look more fashionable. This house in Corve Street (now divided into Nos 103–4) was of the same standard pattern of late sixteenth-century Ludlow. Its framing was then hidden and both of its gables removed. Only quite recently has the framing been exposed again to view.

60 Castle Lodge, on Castle Square, is an intriguing structure with a history going back to medieval times. In the late sixteenth century it was the home of the porter, and then the governor, of the castle. The arched doorway is medieval but the building appears to have been radically rebuilt in stone in the 1580s, when it was the 'fayre house of Maister Sackford'. The timber-framed top storey appears to be a slightly later addition.

storeys, with two gabled bays facing the street. These have a strict hierarchy of framing pattern – close-studding for the ground floor, diagonal bracing for the first, and ornate cusped curving braces in the second. This may or may not have been a deliberate attempt to echo the 'correct' hierarchy of the classical orders.

The domestic arrangements of houses had virtually been set by the start of the seventeenth century – apart from proper bathrooms and fitted kitchens – and most later changes were all to do with architectural fashions. Ludlow's own architectural development virtually came to a halt after the start of the seventeenth century, which is hardly surprising considering the town's history. Several houses were built in the 1650s, but these were mainly to replace others destroyed during the Civil War.

(text continues on p. 85)

61 Inns have always played an important part in the life of market towns, and Ludlow has always had more than its fair share of them. The Bull Ring Tavern is a striking timber-framed composition, but one that, like so many others, was hidden behind plaster for many years until this century.

62 Ludford also had its inns. This was the former Old Bell built alongside the main Worcester road, its porch bearing the date 1614. In the early nineteenth century the local turnpikes were reorganized and the main road was diverted to the west, leaving this part of Ludford isolated on a cul-de-sac.

63 Perhaps the owner of this house in Broad Street wanted the best of both worlds in the eighteenth century. The original attic gables were removed, a new roof added , and the original late sixteenth-century framing was hidden by lath-and-plaster to make the building appear more up to date. However, the ornate carved brackets that supported the jettied gables were left exposed.

64 After 1551 the Corporation appointed a Reader, or lecturer, to carry out some of the duties of the Church. In the eighteenth century the post-holder lived in the Reader's House, at the east side of the churchyard. Mainly of sixteenth-century date, some of the masonry is much older, and the tall three-storey Jacobean porch was added in 1616 by the then chaplain of the Council of the Marches. After years of neglect the house was restored in 1909, and was for a time open to the public.

64 The magnificent doorway in the south porch of the Reader's House shows Jacobean craftsmanship at its most ornate – and this was probably the back door of the property.

65 These modest sixteenth- and seventeenth-century timber-framed buildings are at the northern end of Corve Street, once an important leather-working area. They were restored by the District Council.

The eighteenth century brought rapid change to the external appearances of Ludlow houses, with the arrival of brick – and symmetry. It is virtually impossible in a town like Ludlow to date a building from its façade, as so many façades are exactly that. The occasional clue may be had in the odd arrangements of windows or doorways, fitting in with the timber-framed structure behind, or by the way the brickwork slumps unexpectedly.

No doubt Ludlow, like any other town, had its own appalling slums as well as its grand Georgian houses, but few traces of these have been left. Better housing for the working classes began to appear at the end of the nineteenth century and the start of the twentieth, either through private patronage, such as Clive Cottages in Ludford, or through local councils, such as the short terraces in an estate off Old Street. Only very recently have some of Ludlow's housing estates taken on the blandness that can be seen the length and breadth of England – but the town has been spared the worst.

66 Clive Cottages, in Ludford, are a typical example of a paternalistic landowner providing reasonable accommodation for his workforce in the late nineteenth century. The stone-built terrace was built in a deliberately old-fashioned, neo-vernacular, style.

67 Nos 2–4 Dinham, just outside the castle walls, seems, at first glance to be a standard late sixteenth-century Ludlow house. On closer inspection, something is not quite right about the way the top storey joins on to the rest. The building was radically rebuilt in 1656 after being damaged in the Civil War, hence the oddity in the design.

68 A charter of 1552 transferring the responsibilities of the dissolved Palmers' Gild to the town stated that a public preacher be appointed. In 1611 the Corporation rebuilt this house in Old Street to accommodate the post-holder.

69 Dinham House is the largest Georgian house in Ludlow and one of the few to be set in its own spacious grounds. The central portion was built in the early eighteenth century, the wings being added in 1748. It later became the town house of the Earl of Powis, and Lucien Bonaparte, Napoleon's brother, lived here for six months in 1811 after being captured at sea by the Royal Navy en route for America.

70 The sagging brick front of this house in Bell Lane betrays the fact that the building is actually timber-framed. It was probably refronted in the first half of the eighteenth century and the first floor sashes are of that period.

71 The fashion for symmetrical brick façades led to the refacing of many older properties. If there was enough money, a brick front could be added. A cheaper option was to cover the timber framing with lath and plaster and rearrange the windows. Sometimes, as in these houses in Brand Lane, this is easy to spot: not many brick buildings are jettied!

72 The earliest surviving examples of brick buildings in Ludlow date to the early eighteenth century and Brand House in Brand Lane is probably one of the earliest. Seven bays wide and two storeys high, with dormer-lit attics, it presumably dates to the first two decades of the century. The plate-glass glazing is, obviously, much later. This, together with the painting of the mellow red brickwork, has taken away much of the house's character.

73 The driveway beneath this early brick building leads to Quality Square, a quiet backwater just off the main market-place. Its buildings are of rubblestone and brick and defy architectural description. The façade block itself has obviously seen many changes.

74 It is unusual in towns like Ludlow, where the houses lining the streets are tightly packed together, to be able to see the sides or backs of houses. This fine early Georgian house on Castle Square is a notable exception, dated 1728 on its rain-water hoppers. At the back, the segmental heads of the windows are replaced by flat ones, still with stone keystones. Again, the glazing is not original.

75 The local Silurian limestone was not usually used for the front walls of Georgian houses but there were some exceptions, such as this early eighteenth -century house at the bottom of Mill Lane, just outside the old town walls. Some of the casements may be original – by no means all houses at this date would have been fitted with the more expensive balanced sashes.

76 By far the grandest stone-faced house in the town was refronted by the architect T.F. Pritchard in 1764 for Somerset Davies. No. 27 Broad Street was built in the late seventeenth century for Job Charlton of Ludford, Speaker of the House of Commons. The remodelled façade has lumps of stone little larger than bricks and a central pedimented projection with round-headed stair window echoing grander Palladian buildings. Mercifully the originally glazing bar pattern has survived.

77 Not all the Georgian buildings of Ludlow were fine examples of current architectural taste. This large rubblestone building in Lower Raven Street is very roughly finished indeed and lacks datable features – although it probably belongs to the first half of the century.

78 In contrast, this house in Mill Street is little altered externally, and of fine-quality workmanship. It too probably belongs to the first half of the century. The glazing bars have been kept, which really does enhance the character of the building. They are quite thick, a typical feature of early Georgian sashes.

79 The tripartite Venetian window was popularized in the early eighteenth century by the Palladians and was often used to light stair halls or as the central feature of particular elevations. This astonishing display of Venetian windows in No. 39 Broad Street is not what the Palladians had in mind – but the owner who refronted the house in the third quarter of the eighteenth century clearly felt the more the merrier.

80 The Dinham Hall Hotel, in Dinham, is almost unique in Ludlow as it is faced with ashlared masonry. It was built in 1792 by Samuel Nash, land agent for one of the most important landowners, Richard Payne Knight of Downton Castle – a few miles west of the town. The ashlar suits its rather severe late Georgian style, the rectangularity only relieved by a full-height bow window on the garden front. The deeply recessed windows with their thin glazing bars are typical of the date.

81 The seriousness of Georgian architecture gradually gave way to the much fresher Regency style in the early nineteenth century. Old styles were copied in light-hearted ways. This polygonal lodge, to Ludford House, has mock-Tudor windows and an oversized chimney.

82 Mock-Tudor windows also occur on this delightfully eccentric pair of cottages, Cliff Villas, in Ludford. Virtually every other motif that could be wished for can also be found in a composition that would have had later architectural critics cringing. The cottages probably date to the second quarter of the nineteenth century.

83 Friar's Terrace, in Old Street, is one of the very few terraces built in Ludlow – a town in which the grand late Georgian or Regency row found no favour. This range probably dates from the second quarter of the nineteenth century and took its inspiration from a slightly earlier example higher up the street and on the opposite side.

84 Stone House may seem an odd name to give a building faced with stucco. This pretentious neo-Palladian front in Corve Street probably dates to the 1840s and was added to an earlier eighteenth-century structure built of rubblestone. The composition is not helped by the rather silly porch, and the general impression is of a mediocre provincial bank. Stone House is now part of the headquarters of South Shropshire District Council.

85 Ludlow lacks Victorian buildings of note but, at the same time, has managed to avoid the worst excesses of the nineteenth century. This house on the corner of Castle Square and Dinham is one exception. Its imported fiery red brick and mechanical stonework contrast with the local materials and its style is eclectic, to say the least. Nevertheless, it is certainly a building of character and Ludlow can afford to live with a little bit of bad taste – if only to remind itself of how lucky it is with the rest of its architecture.

86 The Midland Bank of 1905 reflects the taste for the vernacular antique but is a very poor example of it. It does at least have some merit and the craftsmanship employed on it can be appreciated. That is more than can be said for the modern extension with its tiled front; it looks like a public convenience turned inside out: how did they get away with it?

87 It is something of a surprise to come across what must, in the 1930s, have been quite a revolutionary building for Ludlow. In 1936 a new Roman Catholic church, St Peter's, was built in Henley Road in the Byzantine style. The vicarage next door was uncompromisingly modern and a good example of its type.

88 For the past few years, in theory at least, planners have been concerned with ensuring that modern development does not ruin the character of historic towns. In Ludlow, by and large, they have been very successful – using the right building materials and, above all, building to the right scale. These new houses at the bottom of Old Street are typical – the two-storey terrace under a pitched roof follows the line of the street, and the cobbling in front of them is a nice touch. It is just a shame that no more thought was given to the details of the window and door surrounds.

Industrial Buildings

Ludlow, like any important medieval town, had its industries but these have left few visible remains. Many buildings that may well have been industrial once have survived because they have been adapted for other purposes and their original layouts have been lost. Thus it is known that Lower Corve Street was an important area for the leather industries, and Lower Broad Street for the woollen industry, but none of the surviving buildings are easily recognizable as former workshops or stores. One lucky survival is a glove-making workshop in Corve Street, next to Foxe's Almshouses; it looks innocuous enough apart from its rather unusual attic. This was, in fact, the glovers' garret workshop, the only one left in the town, and the whole ensemble probably dates to around 1800. Another small-scale industrial workshop is identified simply by a name plaque on the wall – the nail workshop in Linney.

For centuries the Teme and the Corve provided the water power to turn the waterwheels for Ludlow's fulling and corn mills. The present weirs are probably those noted by Stukeley in the 1720s and may be on sites dating back to medieval times. The mills were a constant source of dispute and anyone from the town using those on the Herefordshire bank could be fined. Mills and their wheels have survived all along the Teme, and there is a particularly fine example at Ashford Carbonel just downstream of Ludlow. In the town itself the survivals are few, the best being Temeside Mill whose waterwheel still powered machinery at the start of the 1930s. Part of the more picturesque Ludford Mill, possibly dating back to the seventeenth century, survives behind the youth hostel on one side of the V-shaped weir below the bridge, but the larger mill on the town bank was recently demolished and the remnants incorporated into new housing.

89 There was a mill in Ludford in Saxon times, and it may even have used a weir on the same site as the present one, just below the bridge. The weirs harnessed the river to power the waterwheels of the fulling and corn mills. Ludford weir is V-shaped, and once served mills on both banks. Part of the seventeenth-century Ludford Mill can be seen just beyond the canoeists. Because of its many weirs the Teme is the best 'whitewater' river in the area.

90 The sorry remains of the waterwheel that, even up to the start of the 1930s powered the Temeside Mill, sits over the mill race.

91 The Temeside Mill was built in the nineteenth century in a mixture of stone and brick with cast-iron framed windows, and until the 1880s was known as the New Mill. Corn milling stopped at around the turn of the century but in 1921 the building reopened as the Temeside Case Mill, turning out cases for jewellery and cutlery. This work stopped in 1931, since when the building has turned out false teeth and wood-burning stoves – and it is still in commercial use.

92 This pleasant but apparently undistinguished building at the Linney Turn off Corve Street is the only complete glover's workshop left in the town. Above the living quarters is a garret workshop with slatted plank sides. The planks could be adjusted for light and ventilation. The building was probably built at around the beginning of the nineteenth century, when the glove-making industry was at its height.

93 Ludlow was an important junction on the turnpike road system and once had several tollgates, each with their tollkeeper's lodges, like this early nineteenth-century example on the junction of Temeside and Friar's Street. Typically octagonal, traditionally to allow the tollkeeper to see traffic arriving in both directions, it was built of rubblestone. The blank window above the doorway probably once contained the toll board.

94 For 900 years Ludlow's main industries have all been directly or indirectly connected with agriculture, and there has probably been a market in the town for all those years. The general market in Castle Square will no doubt continue to thrive, but the future of the Smithfield off Corve Street is less certain. There are outline schemes to move it to a new out-of-town site; which would be a pity. In the background is a fine late nineteenth-century grain warehouse, a reminder of the arable side of agriculture.

Further Reading

Local Books

Faraday, M., *Ludlow 1085–1660: A Social, Economic and Political History* (1991)

Garner, L., *The Buildings of Shropshire: Vol II, The Tudor and Stuart Legacy 1530–1730* (1989)

——, *The Buildings of Shropshire: Vol III, The Georgian and Regency Legacy 1730–1840* (1990)

Lloyd, D., *Broad Street* (1979)

Lloyd, D., & Klein, P., *Ludlow: A Historic Town in Words and Pictures* (1984)

Pevsner, N., *The Buildings of England: Shropshire* (1958)

Scard, M. Ann, *The Building Stones of Shropshire* (1990)

Speight, M.E., and Lloyd, D., *Ludlow Houses and their Residents* (1978)

General Books

Brunskill, R.W., *Timber Building in Britain* (1985)

——, *Brick Building in Britain* (1990)

Clifton-Taylor, A., *The Pattern of English Building* (4th ed. 1987)

Cossons, N., *The BP Book of Industrial Archaeology* (1987)

Cruickshank, D., *A Guide to the Georgian Buildings of Britain & Ireland* (1985)

Harris, R., *Discovering Timber-Framed Buildings* (1978)

Pevsner, N., *The Buildings of England* series, in county volumes

Platt, C., *The English Medieval Town* (1976)

Index

Page numbers in bold indicate illustrations.